Simone Wiemken

You and Your Horse

How to become friends

Simone Wiemken

You and Your Horse
How to become friends

David & Charles

A DAVID & CHARLES BOOK

David & Charles is a subsidiary of F&W (UK) Ltd.,
an F&W Publications Inc. company

First published in the UK in 2004

Distributed in North America
by F&W Publications, Inc.
4700 East Galbraith Road
Cincinnati, OH 45236
1-800-289-0963

A catalogue record for this book is available from the British Library.

ISBN 0 7153 1731 8

Printed in Singapore by KHL Printing Co.
for David & Charles
Brunel House   Newton Abbot   Devon

Visit our website at www.davidandcharles.co.uk

David & Charles books are available from all good bookshops; alternatively
you can contact our Orderline on (0)1626 334555 or write to us at FREEPOST
EX2110, David & Charles Direct, Newton Abbot, TQ12 4ZZ (no stamp required
UK mainland).

Contents

FROM HUMAN

Having a horse

TO HORSE

as a friend

Having a horse as a friend

A good friend puts on a halter with care.

What do you think of when you hear the word 'horsemanship'? Of course, to be a good 'horseman', you have to know a lot about horses, but there's more to it than that. Good horsemanship means having a horse as a friend, and not just looking at him as a piece of sporting equipment for winning competitions. It means treating a horse as something very special, every day — no matter whether the horse is your own or is one that belongs to a riding school.

Good horsemanship shows itself in all the little details of the way you behave with horses — it isn't just a matter of good riding. You can show that you are a good horseman right from the start, in all your daily dealings with horses. For example, how you put on the headcollar or halter. Never forget that your horse is special and shouldn't have to put up with having the halter dragged roughly over his ears, or getting pulled along behind you on the lead rope as if he were made of wood. Instead, use your body to show the horse what you want him to do. In riding, these body signals are called 'aids' and we give them with our legs, our hands, our body weight and our voice. Most horses try hard to do what people want them to do, but they really appreciate being asked nicely and can get stubborn if you try to force them into it.

I WANT MY HORSE TO MOVE OVER !

AN EXAMPLE: You're grooming your horse. He's standing too close to the fence rail, so you need him to step outwards for you to groom his other side. Now, someone with no horsemanship skills might press both their hands on the horse's stomach, shove with all their might and shout, 'Move to the side, you silly animal!'

But you are a good horseman and you can imagine how the 'silly animal' will react to that, can't you? Of course, he'll resist the unpleasant pressure on his stomach by pushing back and crushing the clumsy groom right into the fence.

A better horseman would touch the horse's stomach, lightly and quite quickly, with a fingertip and say in a normal voice, 'Move to the side.' This light prod 'asks' the horse if he would like to take a step to the side. Most horses will do what you ask.

If yours doesn't move, though, don't start shoving him around. Keep making your invitation with your fingertip until he starts to find it annoying and takes a step to the side. This will also teach your horse that there isn't any point in ignoring your wishes, because, even though you don't get angry, you keep asking until you get what you want. Next time you're grooming, your horse will make room for you much more quickly, because he'll have learnt that it's better to obey at once and avoid the annoying prodding.

Practical tip

THE PRINCIPLE OF LIGHT AIDS !

When you are with your horse, and when you're riding, remember the principle of 'light' aids. Whatever you want from your horse, first give a gentle signal, and wait to see what comes of it.

If you always start by giving a light aid, then give stronger and stronger signals if nothing happens, you'll be amazed how attentive and obedient your horse will become in a very short time. However, your light aids must not be timid. You have to know exactly what you want. If your horse goes too quickly when you're leading, lightly tug the lead rope once, and say 'Slowly'. But if you gently pull the rope and at the same time think to yourself, 'I hope you don't run away...' your horse will immediately sense your uncertainty and will be very tempted to make the most of it.

TEST YOUR HORSEMANSHIP ?

Find the answers on pages 72—73.

Tick the answer you think is right.   Yes   No

1. If my horse stops while being led because he's afraid of the stable cat, I should:

a) Jerk the halter sharply and hold the rope shorter.

b) Chase the cat away.

c) Say in a normal voice, 'Don't be silly, it's just Tiddles, you know her,' then walk on.

2. If my horse is always kicking the stable door with a front hoof, I should:

a) Shout at the horse every time he does it, so that in the end he'll learn that it isn't allowed.

b) Make sure the horse gets more exercise.

c) Tie him up in the stable so that he can't reach the door any more.

Tick the answer you think is right.	Yes	No

3. If my horse won't lift his feet, although he knows it's time for them to be cleaned out, I should:

a) Kick the leg my horse is refusing to lift.

b) Hit the joint with the flat of my hand, so that the leg buckles and I can lift the hoof.

c) Wrap my hand around the back of his lower leg and press with my thumb and forefinger on the sinewy part until it becomes annoying to my horse and he raises his hoof.

4. If I go out into the pasture and all the horses start to pester me, I should:

a) Share out fodder so that they leave me alone.

b) Keep eye contact with all the horses and slowly walk away.

c) Wave my arms about wildly to make them go away.

5. I want to jump a fence with my horse, but he runs round it to the right. So...

a) I punish him with my whip, because I know perfectly well that he can jump this height.

b) I put the bar lower and start off by jumping over the little fence.

c) On the next approach, I hold the left rein short, so that he can't break out to the right.

6. I'm riding downhill and my horse starts to trot. So...

a) I let him trot — after all, he should know how to get down a hill!

b) I bring him back to a walk, because I know from experience how easy it is to fall when trotting downhill.

c) I drive him on to a canter so that the hill is over and done with quickly.

HORSES
What do I need to

IN THE HERD

know about horses?

What do I need to know about horses?

Horses are herd animals and they are also flight animals. Almost everyone knows this, but not many people stop to think what these facts actually mean. Like all plant-eaters, or herbivores, horses are a tempting target for predators. In the herd, the horses protect themselves and the other herd members against this danger by being constantly watchful. As soon as one of the horses notices a predator nearby, he will alert the others, and all the horses will take flight.

Our domesticated horses are not threatened by predators. At worst, they might be pestered by naughty dogs. But the problem is that they simply don't know that there aren't any wolves or big cats lurking around. Just like wild horses, they still take fright when they suddenly notice something that might be a predator. You've probably seen this yourself; perhaps your horse has shied away from children playing, someone on a bicycle, a bird in a hedge or a plastic bag in a ditch. Horses don't stop to think sensibly about just what might be in the ditch. First, they get themselves to somewhere that they feel safe, and then they decide whether they dare to go back and look at the object or whether they'd rather not take the risk.

Because a horse has such a strong flight instinct, he can try to run from trouble even with a rider on his back.

Horses might not be threatened by wolves any more, but they do sometimes get chased by cheeky dogs.

Horses will defend themselves

But what happens if a horse can't take flight — for example, if he's in a stable? If a horse becomes very frightened, but can't run away, he will never give up without a struggle. He'll defend himself with his hooves and teeth. A horse that goes for anyone who comes into the stable has probably had bad experiences with people at some time in his life. To begin with, he probably defended himself out of fear, and then he quickly learnt that he could keep people at bay by being really nasty and threatening all the time. Because they are handled by lots of people, some of whom may not be very considerate, a lot of riding school horses use this trick: as soon as you open the stable door, they put their ears back or turn their hindquarters towards you. If a strange horse greets you in this way, don't go into his stable! Ask the riding teacher or groom whether he is only threatening, or if he really does bite or kick.

You'll see playing in the herd, and fighting too.

Watching horses

Next time your horse is with the others out in the paddock, take some time to watch what goes on. You'll soon notice that some horses are more bossy, or dominant, than others. You can see this especially clearly when horses at pasture are given some extra hay. There's always one horse who is the boss, and who thinks that because he's the boss all the hay bales are his own private property. This horse has the highest status among the horses in the field, and is known as the herd leader. The herd leader isn't necessarily the biggest or oldest horse in the group, but will often be the one with the most experience or the bravest.

All members of the herd have their own fixed status in the hierarchy. Sometimes this is quite hard to spot. For example, in one particular group of horses Rebel is the boss. He drives everyone else away from the fodder. But he can't eat everything at once, and so Lottie manages to get a place. Lottie chases off Felix, and Felix chases Tosca away. So, does Tosca go hungry? Not at all — Tosca goes up to Lottie with her ears put back, and takes Lottie's food. This means that in this group Lottie has a higher status than Felix and Felix is stronger than Tosca, but

Tosca has a higher status than Lottie. It all seems pretty complicated, doesn't it?

You're probably thinking how horrible this must be for all the horses apart from Rebel! They've all got a boss in front of their nose who is allowed to push them around whenever he feels like it. But horses don't think like that. In fact, they are only happy when they've found a fixed place in the herd hierarchy, because that gives them the feeling that there's someone there who will protect and look after them. They feel as safe as in a close-knit family, where the parents keep an eye on the children and tell them what they can do and what they can't. When you take your horse out of the pasture, you have to replace his family, and become his herd leader so that he feels safe with you.

Shetland ponies are eager to learn and great for young children.

Warmbloods are 16 or 17 hands (or 1.70 metres) high. They make wonderful dressage and jumping horses.

Are all horses the same?

You're probably thinking, what a stupid question! A Shetland pony looks completely different from a Thoroughbred. But, apart from their outward appearance, all horses are also different inside, in their character. There are lazy horses and hard-working horses, temperamental ones and gentle ones. Up to a point, a horse's temperament is decided by his breed. For example, Arabs are mostly more temperamental than New Forest ponies. But it's important to remember the 'mostly' — because you can't depend on it. There are also laid-back Arabs — and Shetlands that don't seem to have any brakes! Generally,

Arab horses are often fast, and are ideal for riding over long distances.

though, you can assume that finely bred horses, such as Arabs, thoroughbreds and their cross-breds, get upset more quickly than the more robust breeds like Highlands, Haflingers, Shetlands or Dartmoors.

WHAT TYPE IS MY HORSE **?**

Tick the answer that fits best.　　Yes　Sometimes　No

Does your horse shy when you're riding in the indoor school and another rider's stirrup knocks against the wall?

Does your horse get upset if you want to ride at a walk in the paddock or the school, while the other riders are cantering?

While you're riding, are you always having to hold your horse back to stop him going too fast?

When you're leading, does your horse walk nicely beside you, without pulling?

After shying, is your horse still nervous and tense several minutes later?

When the other horses are charging about in the pasture, does yours join in?

Does he get very upset if you ride past a paddock where other horses are galloping about?

Does he often skip and jog when he should be walking?

Does he shy away from things that don't bother the other horses?

Find the answers on pages 73—74.

Horses sniff at each other over the fence when they first meet.

How do horses communicate with each other?

In horsey adventure stories, the lead stallion always warns his herd of impending danger with plenty of loud neighing. Western movies are full of neighing, too. But in reality, horses don't neigh very much at all — really only when they feel lonely. For example, if you take a horse's stable companion away, he'll call after it for a while, and he may call again when he hears you coming back.

Rather than neighing when they have something to communicate, horses 'talk' to each other silently, using their body posture. You'll probably have seen some of this body language yourself. For example, when a horse puts his ears back he is telling another horse, or you, 'I'm angry with you!' or simply 'Get out of my way!' Ears pricked and an interested face make a horse look as though he's saying, 'Who are you then?', which is pretty much what he's thinking. And the tail can tell you a great deal, too. For example, if it is held high with the root pointing upwards, it means that the horse is feeling high-spirited. However, if a horse lashes his tail around, it can mean that he's unhappy about something, and if his tail is clamped between his hindlegs, it's a sign of fear — and it's a danger signal for you, because a frightened horse may kick. Another danger signal is a hindleg raised threateningly.

Horses rarely bother to attack their pasture companions. Each member of the herd already knows its place in the hierarchy, and if one does dare to attempt to get a better position, when they're all eating hay for example, all the higher-status horse has to do is make a threatening lash of his tail or raise a hindleg and this soon puts the upstart back in his place. In most cases, as soon as a higher-status horse starts to move towards a lower-status one, the lesser one will make room.

Exercise at grass and among companions is vital for horses.

Foals learn horse behaviour by playing.

Observing foals, and learning the language of horses

Do you know anyone who breeds horses? If so, find some time to go and watch the foals and young horses when they're out in the fields. Youngsters are much livelier than the brood mares and riding horses, and by watching them, you can see especially clearly how horses communicate with each other. The colts often play fighting games or they might race the fillies, which is something you rarely see among older horses. For races to start, it's enough for one of the foals to raise his tail vertically and trot with light steps towards another one. This is a challenge to a contest. Another clear signal is one foal going towards another with his upper lip stretched forward. This tells the second foal that the first foal's coat is itching and he would like to be scratched. You often see adults grooming one another's coats like this, too.

If the foals are fed at a single big trough, you can get a wonderful idea of how the status system works. The high-status foals push ruthlessly between those that are already feeding and barge them to one side. Those that have been pushed away from the trough will then try to find themselves another place by pushing between two even lower-status foals, playing the same game with them. And, until foals learn that people are higher-status creatures, they'll treat us in exactly the same way as their fellow horses: they'll barge into us, kick at us and sometimes even bite.

Serious fights never happen between foals, but they can break out among adult horses when a new horse that doesn't yet have a place in the hierarchy joins the herd. If this horse has been used to having a high status in his previous group, he will want a similar place in this new group, too, and, of course, that won't please the existing bosses. This means that there will be a battle for status between the newcomer and the herd leader. Usually, the herd leader will win, and after that, the newcomer will have to fight with the other horses for a place in the hierarchy.

Status fights are very dangerous, especially if the horses are shod. To avoid injury, newcomers should not be turned out with the other horses straight away. The best solution is to put the new horse in the paddock next door for a few days, so that the established horses can snuffle at him over the fence and get to know him. Then when he joins them in their own field, any status tussles will be a lot less aggressive.

ALWAYS TAKE CARE !

Do not walk into a paddock of foals if you aren't sure whether they have learnt that people are higher-status creatures. And it goes without saying that you must never enter anyone else's paddock without getting their permission first.

RELIABLE

How can I become my

FRIEND
horse's herd leader?

HOW can I become my horse's herd leader?

When you go out to catch a horse, approach him slowly and with determination.

Horses need someone to tell them what to do and what not to do. Within the herd, this job is done by the herd leader, who can be a mare, a gelding or a stallion. When you are with your horse, you must become the substitute for the herd leader. This means that you must behave in such a way that the horse understands you. While observing the herd, you've probably noticed that the boss doesn't need to use violence to rule his underlings. He doesn't need to bite them or hit them — they obey him, because they respect him. This should be your goal with your horse — that he respects you and does what you ask of him without being scared of you. Of course, you can make a horse do what you want by shouting at or hitting him, but this won't make the horse respect people, instead he will be frightened of them. That's no good to us — we want the horse to be our friend.

CONFIDENCE IS IMPORTANT !

Gaining a horse's respect depends on your self-confidence. Someone who is always being rough with their horse or shouting at it usually lacks confidence in themselves, and is secretly afraid of horses, too.

This fear usually shows up in that person's horse. If you reach out to stroke him, he'll jerk his head back in fear, and if you walk towards him, he'll jump quickly to the side.

How can I tell whether my horse respects me?

This is a difficult question to answer. To find out if your horse respects you, you need to keep a close eye on him as you spend time with him each day.

If your horse respects you, you'll notice that he will make room for you when you work around him without you having to ask. Respectful horses also get out of the way when you muck out their stable, and if they're being groomed, they move to the side of their own accord when it's time for you to change sides. As mentioned earlier (page 9), you can get your horse to do this.

RESPECT IN THE PADDOCK, TOO !

Does your horse stand quietly while you put a headcollar on him in the paddock? If yes, then you have his respect.

But, if he goes on peacefully grazing, while you pull at his mane trying to get him to lift his head for a second so you can put the halter on, he's showing you that he's indifferent to you. Make it clear that this isn't acceptable. Loop the lead rope around his neck and pull hard, once. The pressure on his windpipe is so unpleasant to the horse that he'll raise his head. And that very moment is when you praise him.

Practical tip

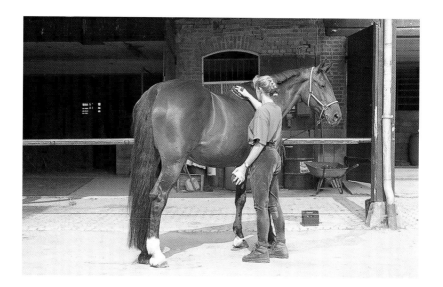

The way you behave when you groom your horse tells him whether he should respect you, or not.

When you groom or muck out, make your requests again and again, until it becomes a habit for your horse to move out of your way. In the beginning, you might have to use a lot of energy to make him understand that you want some room, but after a while a light touch of the finger will be enough to signal to him to move aside.

Basically, it can be said that your horse respects you if he pays attention to you. If he notices something interesting while he is being groomed, it's fine for him to turn his head and look. But if he swings his whole body round and delivers you such a thump with his hindquarters that you're sent flying into the muck heap, that's almost always a sign of lack of respect. 'Almost always', because even the very best-behaved horse sometimes takes fright.

It's important to learn to tell the difference between fear and lack of respect. If your horse knocked you over from fear — in other words, by mistake — it would be unfair to give him a furious smack on the backside for it. That would only give him yet another fright. You can only do one thing: grit your teeth and pretend that nothing has happened. But if you already know

Many horses enjoy being groomed with a soft brush.

that your horse is a bit of a hooligan, then all the time you're with him you should be wide awake, ready to nip all his bad manners in the bud.

However, don't make the mistake of constantly nagging a horse that behaves like this. Don't tolerate things that are dangerous to you — firmly stop things like barging, shoving and trampling on your feet. But apart from that, you need come to terms with your horse's basically insensitive nature, and instead find good opportunities to praise him. If all you ever do is moan at him, he'll soon stop listening to you. Learn to weigh up what you find lovable in his character, and what you don't.

For example, after a ride, a lot of riders let their horses enjoy rubbing their sweaty head against them. They think that this is a sign of the trust and affection that exists between them and their horse. Really, though, their horse would show the same 'respect' to a nice big tree branch, if there was one within reach. When a horse rubs his head on the rider, this is not proof of trust, but a sign of disrespect — the horse would never be allowed to do this to another horse of higher status. So don't let your horse do it to you — apart from everything else, it's very dangerous.

This horse has learnt not to be afraid of a flapping plastic sheet!

Just imagine if your horse butted his head into your face by mistake! If your horse is an enthusiastic head-rubber, you can do him the favour first and rub his head for him. But you must be the one to offer this sort of attention, and during the rubbing, he must keep his head away from you. That makes it better for both of you, rather than you constantly pushing his head away when he swings it in your direction.

Do I have to whisper to horses?

Recently everyone's been talking about 'horse whisperers', or people who can tame even the wildest of horses. Some of these whisperers make a lot of fuss about this supposed 'art' of theirs, but they don't let you know anything about the trick that they're using. And, in most cases, it isn't a trick at all. These men and women are really just people who have learnt to handle all kinds of horses in all kinds of different ways.

There have always been horse 'whisperers'. In the past they were often unpleasant people who used force to make horses see that there was no point in resisting humans. Today, for the most part, horse training is much more sensible, and kinder to the horse. During training the horse learns that humans are not dangerous, and that he doesn't need to run away if he gets frightened. A good example of this sort of horse training is called 'sacking out'.

In sacking out, a horse is stroked with a soft cloth. Then, gradually, the trainer begins to flap the cloth about a little. As the horse accepts what is happening and settles down, the demands on him are increased — the cloth is flapped more vigorously. It's very important that the horse stays calm. The idea is not to make him anxious or frightened, because a frightened horse can not learn anything. During this exercise, he should learn that what the human is doing is not at all dangerous, and doesn't hurt either.

And what's the point of sacking out, you may ask? Well, imagine you want to take off your jacket while you're riding and you have to do this on a horse that hasn't learnt that flapping things are harmless! Now, imagine trying it on a horse that has been forced to get used to flapping things — he will probably bolt in panic, because he's never really learnt that flapping things are safe. All he can remember is the terrible fear he felt the last time,

To teach a horse to have no fear of plastic sheeting...

...takes a lot of work!

But with calmness and trust, this exercise can be successful!

The horse has to learn to give way to an aid given with the whip.

RESPECT WITHOUT FORCE

Test whether your horse reacts to you in the same way that it would to a higher-status horse. Put on his halter then stand about a metre (3 feet) in front of his head holding him on a loose rope, draw yourself up to your full height and look in his eyes. Now, start walking towards him — the idea is to make him walk backwards because this is the best way of seeing whether he respects you. Make a definite forward step. At the same time, you must think, 'I want to be where you are standing. So move back!' This is very important. You need to show as much authority as the herd leader. If your horse doesn't react, you need to be clearer — the leader would do the same if its underlings didn't obey. Swing the lead rope gently this way and that, and raise your whip, so that the horse understands that this puny little person in front of him is really worthy of his respect. If you can successfully make your horse walk backwards whenever you like, just by your manner and your aura, then you've taken your first step towards becoming a horse whisperer.

Once you've mastered walking backwards, see if you can get your horse to give way sideways. For that, you need to walk towards his shoulder, at an angle from the front. By this time he needs to have learnt that you are someone who has something to say. If it doesn't work, swing the lead rope again and raise the whip until the horse moves to the side.

Practical tip

and he reacts accordingly — by trying to run away.

So by now you should have realized that the old method of using force didn't really work very well. It only succeeded in filling the horse with anxiety and fear. You can learn a lot from the horse whisperers of today who 'speak' to horses in the horse's own language. The secret of their success is that they act as if they were horses of a higher status. And this isn't as difficult as it sounds. It helps if you observe how horses behave among themselves. For example, when a higher-status horse moves towards another one, wanting it to make room, he approaches at an angle from behind. This is the driving position.

Horses react very well to human body language.

If he wants the other one to get out of the way, he moves towards his shoulder at an angle from the front.

COMMUNICATING WITH BODY LANGUAGE !

For the next exercise, you need a small, fenced-in space — a lungeing ring or round pen would be ideal, but an ordinary riding arena will do fine. Only do these exercises at a time when you can have the place to yourself. Let your horse loose in the lungeing ring (without a lunge rein on), and stand in the middle. Now experiment to find out how you should stand if you want the horse to run faster or slower, and what you have to do to get him to change direction.

To drive him on — as he goes past you, move your shoulder that is closer to his hindquarters in his direction and walk a few steps with him. Do you notice how he speeds up? That's because you are now in the driving position. To slow him down — as he comes towards you, move the shoulder that is closer to his head in his direction and take a step forwards. This is the braking position. The horse now has the feeling that you are blocking his way, although the distance between you could be up to four metres (12 feet). Depending on how sensitive he is, he will now either halt for a moment before going on, or he may turn round in a flash and run in the opposite direction.

If your horse is not particularly sensitive, and doesn't react to your body language, you have to be clearer. For example, to stop him, move your shoulder in the direction of his head, run a step forward and at the same time stamp down with the foot that is under your forward shoulder. By doing this, you can get even quite a stubborn horse to halt and turn round. But be careful, and stay in the middle of the space, especially if you don't have a lunge ring to practise in but are using a square arena.

If you have halted your horse in a corner, after a few seconds let him go by stepping back. You must never go so close to his hindquarters that he can kick you. Horses that are used to thinking of humans as lower-status creatures sometimes react with outrage when they realize that these funny little two-legged things are suddenly making trouble. If you don't feel confident to do these exercises with a free-running horse, ask your riding teacher or someone else who knows a lot about horses if they will show you how it's done.

Practical tip

Only give your horse treats as a reward for doing something good.

Are treats allowed?

In a lot of stables, it's completely against the rules to give the horses anything from your hand. There are good reasons for this. For one thing, it stops the popular horses from getting more treats than are good for them, and for another, it stops the horses getting the idea that their riders are always going to be slipping them something. When horses start to expect treats as a regular thing, they can become very pushy and demanding, especially if no treat is forthcoming.

However, if you have your own horse, or look after a horse that only or nearly only has contact with you, then it's up to you if you want to spoil him with treats. If your horse respects you, then giving him occasional treats isn't going to cause any trouble. But that doesn't mean you should just fill his mouth with the finest things all the time without ever even thinking about it. Use treats as a reward, and only give the horse one when he has done something really good. Don't try to bribe your horse with goodies.

Horses don't have a guilty conscience. They don't think that they should behave better just because you give them a whole bag of treats — they simply don't think that way. Say you give a horse a treat when you tack him up, by the time you're sitting in the saddle, he will have already forgotten all about it. But a better time to give your horse a treat would be immediately after you've mounted — to reward him for standing still.

Whether or not you reward your horse with treats at all depends on how he behaves. After one treat, many horses become so greedy that they won't work with you any more, because they're only thinking about their next treat. In this case, stop feeding treats for the time being, because it's impossible to practise anything with your horse's head stuck in your pocket. It's up to you to decide if the horse is begging too much. A lot of people can't stand it if their horse is always nudging them, or greets them in the morning with its head on one side and a pleading expression on its face. But, if it doesn't bother you, and as long as your horse isn't using his teeth to 'persuade' you to dole out goodies, then it's fine for you to give him something nice if he's done something good. And, needless to say, whatever you give, always present it on the palm of your hand, so that the horse doesn't get hold of your fingers by mistake. Almost as important, though, you must give the horse the treat without being too obvious about it. Any other horses in the area must not see that yours has been given something.

If your horse is one of those that make you fear for your fingers every time you feed from your hand, then you could bring a little bowl with you and feed him from the bowl before taking him back to the paddock or stable. This way, you can reward him, without encouraging his pushiness.

If you feed your horse from a bowl, he won't be constantly nibbling every pocket of your jacket.

CAN YOU RECOGNIZE HORSE ILLNESSES ?

Find the answers on pages 74—77.

You love your horse, and you enjoy giving him treats. Well, there's nothing wrong with that! But taking care of a horse doesn't only mean that you have a lot of fun. It also means that you have a huge responsibility. Horses can get ill, and you should know how to spot a sick horse and what to do about it. Not sure you're up to it? Do this quiz, to find out!

1. How can I tell if my horse has colic?

_____

_____

2. What should I do if he has colic?

_____

_____

3. What is the normal body temperature of a horse and how is it measured?

_____

_____

4. My horse is coughing — what should I do?

_____

_____

5. What injections does my horse need?

_____

_____

6. How many times a year should I worm my horse?

_____

_____

7. How can I tell if my horse is lame?

_____

_____

8. Can I ride my horse if his back is wet because of rain?

_____

_____

9. How can I tell when it's time to call the farrier?

_____

_____

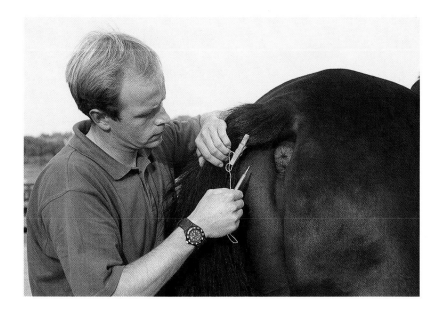

If you think your horse might be feeling ill, take his temperature to be on the safe side.

Catching a horse

When you go out to catch your horse in the field, don't carry the halter over your arm or stretched out in front of you, or he will see that it's time to work. Instead, hang the halter over your shoulder and only bring it down when you're standing next to him. As you approach, keep a watch on what he's doing with his ears. If he lays them back, then beware — it may mean he'll try to avoid being caught. When watching, though, be careful not to look him directly in the eye. Direct eye contact is uncomfortable for many horses, and often makes them move

APPROACHING IN THE RIGHT WAY

When you go up to your horse, whether he's standing in the paddock or in his stable, or is tied up outside being groomed, never ever approach directly from the front or from behind. Only ever approach from the side. Then he will see you coming and won't be surprised or feel threatened.

When you want to get a horse in from the field, pay attention to the whole herd.

backwards out of respect. Instead, look at his shoulder; you'll automatically be able to see his ears at the same time. When you reach him, put the rope round his neck first. This means that you can hold on to him if he decides to walk off. Once you've eased the halter over his head, you can give him a treat if you want to, but don't let the other horses see you do it!

Practical tip

KEEP LOOKING AROUND !

Make sure you always keep an eye on the other horses while you're busy with your own. Even if you know that they're all generally well-behaved, one of them might be in a bad mood, and start to pick a fight with the others — maybe even yours. You need to see this before it actually happens, because once the other horse has bitten yours on the bottom, you will have a problem. Watch the other horses near you closely. Do you see one of them putting their ears back or looking in your direction with flared nostrils and a nasty expression on their face? If you do, then you need to do something at once. Often it's enough to speak to a horse firmly, saying their name. This will show them that you have noticed what they were about to do, and that impresses horses so much that they almost always change their plans. But if you aren't paying attention and the ill-tempered horse actually bites yours on the backside, then it's too late. You can shout at the naughty horse as much as you like, but you can't undo what's done. Remember to act before anything happens, not react after. By doing this, you'll also get a lot of respect from the other horse, who will see you as someone of a higher status than him who stops every squabble before it breaks out.

Leading a horse properly

Nearly all riders have to lead their horses somewhere every day. They bring them in from the paddock, take them out of the stable to be groomed or walk with them while they graze. Usually, it isn't something you have to think about — you pull on the horse's halter and march off. But some horses behave particularly badly when they have the halter on. You can find out whether your horse is one of these by doing this quiz.

IS MY HORSE A PROBLEM TO LEAD?

Tick the answers that fit best. | Yes | No

How well does your horse behave when you're leading him in a halter?

1. I have to pull my horse behind me on the rope.

2. He won't trot when I want to lead him at a trot.

3. He won't stop when I want him to.

4. When I'm leading him, he goes so fast that I have to loosen the rope.

5. Whenever he sees grass, he puts his head down to graze, even if I try to stop him.

6. When I stand in his way, he nudges me aside.

7. He often pulls away from me while being led and then runs off.

8. He pulls his head away from me, tenses his neck and just runs off.

9. He's more difficult to lead from the right than the left.

10. He won't walk backwards on the halter.

Find the answers on pages 42—46.

A horse should be just as easy to lead from the right as from the left.

If you've answered 'yes' to even just one of these questions, you need to practise leading your horse. It's best to do the leading exercises described here in a fenced-off area, so that it isn't too serious if your horse runs off. You should wear gloves, because it is very painful if the lead rope gets pulled through your hands. You already know that you must wear good, solid shoes — never sandals or trainers — when you're with horses, as well as a hard hat, and that you must never ever wind the lead rope around your hand. If you're using a long rope or a lunge rein, make large loops in the end so that they can't catch on your hand. Now all you need is a long schooling whip, and you're ready to start.

Problems 1 and 2 Your horse has to be pulled to make him walk. This problem is easy to solve. Stand next to your horse, roughly where his shoulder meets his neck. Hold the rope in your right hand, around 20 centimetres (8 inches) below his chin, and take the end of the rope in your left hand. The left hand is also holding the whip. Now, give a clear command to walk on — decide on a command and stick to it every time from now on. For example, say 'Walk on!' If he doesn't move, give him a tap on the hindquarters with the whip. But don't look round. Keep looking ahead. It's best to practise giving this tap behind your back without the horse there first. When you touch him with the whip, the horse will go. Walk with him and don't hold him back. If he starts to slow up, repeat the command and give him another tap with the whip. Don't allow him to fall back into pulling along mode again. The same applies to trotting on the lead rope. Choose a command ('Trrrott!') and use the whip like when asking him to walk.

Problems 3 and 4   If your horse won't stop when he's being led, stop moving yourself, say 'Stop!' or 'Halt!' and hold the handle of the whip in front of his face. (To do this, you'll need to be holding the whip in the middle.) If your horse doesn't react to this, give him a gentle tap on the bridge of his nose with the whip. Practise this until he stops when you do. Don't go back to doing leading exercises at the trot until you've got him to understand that the whip in front of his nose means 'Stop'. As soon as he starts to go too quickly, hold up the whip.

Problems 5 and 6   If you have these leading problems, then your horse sees you as another horse of lower status than himself. He does what he likes, and, if you get in his way, you'll

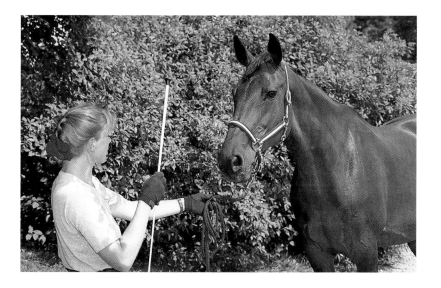

Giving a clear 'stop' signal with the whip.

Use the whip when practising leading, so that the horse learns not to overtake.

get pushed aside. In this sort of situation, an ordinary halter and lead rope are not enough to get him to understand that you're the boss, but a knotted halter can help. (This is also called a Parelli halter, after its inventor, the horse trainer Pat Parelli.) It is made of thin rope and has knots tied in it at certain points. You also need to knot it to fix it on the horse's head, because it doesn't have a buckle. A long and very heavy rope is attached to the halter to be used for leading. Because the halter is very light, the knots form a web of pressure points on the horse's head. When you pull on the rope, or swing it, the knots press on the horse's head and he can feel them very easily. Wait until your horse acts as if you aren't there, and tries to wander off to the nearest tussock of grass, and then just pull on the line, lightning-fast. Most horses are used to broad, softly padded halters, and know that it doesn't hurt if they set themselves against the halter. Although the Parelli halter doesn't hurt either, the pressure point action of the knots surprises the horse just like a finger snapping against his nose would. And that makes sure that his attention comes back to you and your wishes, and he forgets what he originally wanted to do.

Problems 7 and 8   Is your horse usually good when you lead him, only pulling loose when he shies away from something? In this case, a longer rope or a lunge rein might be the solution.

Lead your horse as usual, and carry the long, looped end of the rope or lunge rein in your left hand. If your horse takes fright and runs away, let one or two loops run out and then grip the rope. Allow the horse run on for a metre or two (3–6 feet). That lets him react to his fear, and when he stops, he will see that you are standing there quite calmly — in other words, he sees that things are not as bad as he thought, because his human boss is quite obviously not afraid.

It's a different matter if your horse has got into the habit of running away at the slightest provocation. In this case, if you give him a metre or two more line, you won't be able to stop him at all. In this situation, you should use the Parelli halter (see the explanation on page 44) and, by pulling lightly, ensure that the horse always has his neck slightly inclined towards you while he's walking. Don't let him turn his head away or barge into you with his shoulder.

Problem 9   Most horses are more difficult to lead from the right than from the left. This is because they've been trained to be led from the left since they were little foals. And, as most people are right-handed, it feels more natural for us to lead from the left as well. But, apart from the fact that it's more comfortable, there's no reason only to lead horses from the left. If you want to be able to do it equally well on both sides, there's only one thing for it: practice.

USING A PARELLI HALTER PROPERLY

The thin line halter is good for practising leading. However, you must never tie up your horse with a Parelli halter, because the thin line will cut in painfully if he takes fright and pulls on the rope. Always use an ordinary halter when tying up your horse.

Problem 10 If your horse won't walk backwards on the halter, this means that he doesn't see you as a higher-status animal. He's more or less saying, 'Why should I move back out of your way? Who do you think you are?' To convince him that you're actually the boss, you have to make yourself really big. Stand in front of him and, looking straight at him, draw yourself up to your full height, put your shoulders back, let the rope out a little longer and swing it forcefully to and fro. At the same time, say in a powerful voice, 'Go back!' If that doesn't work, raise the whip with your other hand. As soon as the horse so much as shifts his weight backwards, take a step towards his head, as if to say, 'I want to be exactly where you are standing. So move back!' If he takes a step backwards, praise him, then lead him a metre or two (3-6 feet) forwards. Don't practise walking backwards for too long — one or two steps at a time will be enough. If you do any more than this your horse will think he's being punished.

Making a horse braver

If you have a horse that often shies, you can train him to be braver. To do this, get together as many things as you can find that your horse thinks are scary, like a big plastic sheet, a thick branch with a rope tied to it, a fluttering ribbon (for example, the red and white plastic ribbons used for marking off building sites — you can buy these at a DIY store) or maybe the farmyard dustbin. Again, it's important to do these exercises in a safely fenced-in area.

If you have a very anxious horse, don't expect him to do all the exercises described here in a single day. Do a different one every day, or spend several days doing just one exercise, particularly if he finds it very difficult or scary. Let him have a rest between exercises. Try to finish off a session of exercises by doing something positive that he is really good at, even if it's only something small.

Stand your horse in the enclosure and start putting together your 'obstacles'. Ask a friend to help you. Spread the plastic sheet out on the ground and weigh down the corners with stones so that it doesn't blow away. Put the other objects all around the enclosure. Use the ribbon to build a 'fluttering gateway'. Stretch a string between two poles so that it's at least half a metre (20 inches) higher than the height of the horse. Now tie pieces of ribbon to the string between the poles to make a fluttering curtain.

In the meantime, the horse will have been looking with interest at what you're doing. Lead him across to the plastic sheet and then over it. He doesn't want to go? Give him time. Lead him as close to the sheet as you can. Then let him stand there, while you talk to your friend. In this way, you're killing two birds with one stone: your horse can see that the sheeting really can't be dangerous, otherwise you wouldn't be chatting with your friend, would you? — and he also gets time to think. Gradually, step by step, move closer to the sheeting. All the time you should act as if there isn't any sheeting there at all and talk quietly to your friend. That tells the horse that he isn't the centre of attention so that takes the pressure off him, and, most

The 'fluttering gateway' and plastic sheeting exercises need patient training.

importantly, it tells him that he doesn't have to walk over any plastic sheeting — you're not actually asking him to. Just act as if you're going for a walk, and let your horse accompany you. If he sees through your trick and refuses to walk with you, walk in circles around the sheeting. When this brings you close enough, ask your friend to step onto the sheeting so that the horse hears what sort of noise it makes. If at any point he trusts himself to walk onto the sheeting, reward his bravery with a treat.

If your horse simply won't walk on to the sheet, be content with small amounts of progress and be prepared to take quite a long time to teach him. Lead him in the direction of the sheeting, as near as he wants to go, give him a treat and lead him away again. If you get one step closer the next day, give him a treat again and lead him away. Don't be tempted to overdo it. One day you'll have worked your way right up to the sheeting, and your scaredy-cat of a horse will be so brave that he'll go and fetch his own treat — right off the plastic sheeting!

With the fluttering gateway, you have to do things a bit differently. Get your friend to grab about half of the plastic ribbons and hold them to the side, so that a big gap appears which you can lead the horse through. Make sure that your helper isn't standing in the way because a lot of horses hurry quite smartly between the poles — they tend to follow the principle of 'Shut your eyes and go for it!' Keep doing the exercise until you can lead your horse slowly through all the hanging ribbons.

Next it's time to use the branch. Many horses become frightened when something moves behind them. So start this exercise by getting your friend to pull the branch while you follow behind it with the horse. Your horse is sure to find that very exciting. The next step is for your friend to walk diagonally behind your horse while pulling the branch. Make sure that your friend is far enough from the horse's hindquarters so that there's no danger of being kicked. Once your horse is calmly taking this in his stride, you can hold the rope that is attached to the branch and drag it behind you as you lead him.

When you approach the dustbin (many horses find dustbins terrifying), just behave as you did with the plastic sheeting. Once your horse is brave enough to take a treat that is sitting on the dustbin lid, you can be sure that the 'dustbin monster' won't frighten him again. Try taking the dustbin by the handle and dragging it beside your horse while you lead him. If it doesn't work first time, you'll need your friend to help you again. Build up to dragging it yourself like you did with the branch.

Now, once your horse does all of these exercises calmly, you need to use your imagination. Don't bore him with everlasting plastic sheet or branch-dragging exercises. Think of something new. How about getting your friend to stand in the arena with an umbrella and walking your horse past? Lots of horses hate umbrellas. Or do all the exercises again, this time leading your horse from the right. Can you halt your horse while he's going through the fluttering ribbons? Will he walk backwards through the fluttering gateway? The variations are endless!

DO IT A LITTLE AT A TIME !

If your horse just won't walk over the plastic sheeting, you'll need two narrower sheets of plastic. Lay them a little apart, and lead your horse between them. If that goes well, put them a little closer together. Next, lay them at an angle, so that they touch at one corner. Bit by bit, let them overlap more, until at last they are touching all along their length. Don't forget to praise your horse for his bravery each time!

Practical tip

RIDING WITH

How to be

FEELING

a better rider

How to be a better rider

How to mount

There are various ways of mounting a saddled horse. The method you use depends on what kind of horse you have and what type of saddle it is wearing. With a fairly big horse that is fitted with an English-style saddle, stand so that your left shoulder is next to the left shoulder of the horse — in other words, you face in the opposite direction to the horse. Take the reins in your left hand, directly in front of the saddle, and also grip the horse's mane. Then lift your left leg and put the stirrup onto your foot with your right hand. Now push yourself off the ground with your right foot, grip the cantle of the saddle on the

With big horses you might need a 'leg up'.

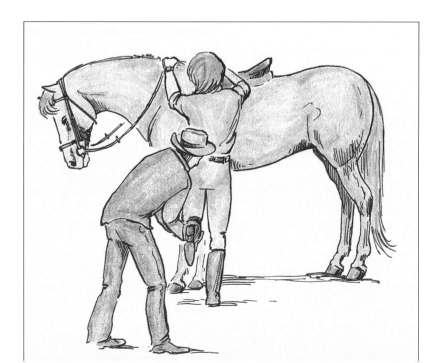

far side of the horse with your right hand, and swing elegantly into the saddle. With a small horse wearing an English saddle, you also mount in the same way, or you could try mounting in the Western fashion, as you would with any horse that is fitted

Mounting is easier when you have a Western saddle or a small horse.

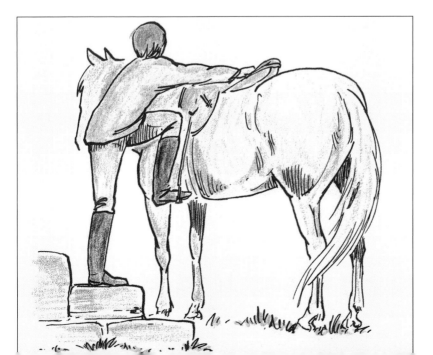

You can also make mounting easier by stepping up on something.

53

with a Western saddle. In this case, stand behind the stirrup but facing the horse. Take the reins in your left hand again, also getting hold of a good handful of mane, or of the pommel on the front of the Western saddle. Now put your left foot in the stirrup, push off the ground with your right foot and simply swing your right leg up and over the saddle to seat yourself. With any method of mounting, it is kinder to the horse, and easier for you, to use a mounting block. This way you can get on more gently without pulling on the horse's back.

Horse and rider in perfect harmony.

Imagine yourself
riding on, then
give the aid!

Two keys to good riding

Have you sometimes admired other riders, asking yourself how
they can look so effortless, and how they get their horses to do
everything they want? Well, riding like them doesn't have to be
as hard as you might think. To do it, you need to remember two
important things.

1. You must know what you want.   Don't be discouraged
if your horse is a lazybones-type who never seems to want
to take a step. If you act as if he is a really wonderful horse, then
he will become one. But if you're constantly tugging on his
bit, and always kicking your heels into his ribs, he'll just get
more and more stubborn. What you have to do is think first, and
then get a picture in your head of what you want your horse
to do next.

For example, say you're riding at a walk and want to trot on.
Please don't just ambush your horse with a sudden poke with
your heels. First, imagine both of you trotting, next sit upright
and heavy in the saddle, then press your lower leg once, lightly,

Don't simply pull on the reins, but instead give careful and correct aids!

against the horse. He probably won't react at first, because he'll be used to quite different tactics, but if you keep the image of both of you at the trot in your mind's eye, and repeat the aid, it's sure to work. If he still doesn't go into trot, you are not on any account to become rough again. Repeat the aid again, and at the same time, give him a light tap with the whip. Once you've done this a few times, before long you'll have a horse that trots the moment you think about it — and your idle old lazybones will have become a sensitive riding horse. But from now on you must remember to do this each time you want him to trot.

2. You must never pull on the reins. Never forget that your horse has a piece of metal in his mouth, to which the reins are attached. If you pull the reins — whether it's one of them, to turn, or both, to stop — it hurts your horse, and horses are in the habit of resisting pain. This means that as soon as you start to pull, so will your horse. And if you compare the strength of your arms with the strength of your horse's neck, you can easily see who's going to win that tug-of-war. But how else are you going to give orders to an animal ten times as heavy as you? Quite simple — you use your brain! Imagine this situation: you want to ride out with your friends, but even before you begin your hack, your horse puts his head down and starts to graze at the side of the track. That makes you cross, so you bend down over the front of your saddle and pull on the reins with all your might. But your horse is very greedy, and ignores you completely. You've lost the battle. You've tried using force, you've achieved nothing and you've lost your temper. It would have been much more sensible to have a think first, and find a way to win. For example, you could drive your horse on while he's grazing. He should react to this impulsively by lifting his head for a moment and taking a step forward. And you can use that moment to take up the reins so he can't get his head down again. There! You've solved

Look in the direction you want to ride in!

the problem without wasting your strength or hurting your horse's mouth. Remember this each time he does something similar. After all, you're the one who's in charge! The more often you take control quietly but firmly, the less often he will misbehave.

A nice canter on a left lead.

Stopping

You may ask, 'How am I supposed to stop or turn my horse if I'm not allowed to pull on the reins?' Well, that's simple too — all it requires is a bit of concentration. Let's look at stopping first. If you're sitting softly on your horse, he will be moving you. If you're at walk, the movement is a gentle swinging; if you're trotting or cantering, the movement is livelier. As long as you want your horse to keep going in the same gait, you keep letting your body follow this movement. And, when you want to stop, stop following! Let both the reins go slack, breathe out and let your weight 'sink into' the horse. This is called 'sitting heavy' in riding language. It's important that you keep your hands still while you're doing it.

It's a similar procedure if you want your horse to slow down. You mustn't pull on the reins either. For example, if you're in a rising trot, and your horse is going faster and faster, try rising and sitting more slowly. Your rising rhythm tells your horse precisely what speed you want him to trot at, and so if you start to rise in a slower rhythm, he will know straight away that he should trot more slowly.

The horse should stop without you pulling on the reins.

Turning

Now to turning or 'steering' the horse. You probably have already learnt how to ride a turn: take up the inside rein, inside leg pushing on the girth, outside leg safely behind the girth. There's a lot to remember and it all seems pretty complicated, doesn't it? Be honest, you usually forget something when you do a turn, don't you? But it doesn't have to be like that — turning is as easy as blinking. All you need to remember is that you have to turn yourself in the direction you want the horse to turn in. Try

If you sit correctly, you will be telling the horse where you want him to go.

it right now, off the horse. Get yourself in your riding position and turn your upper body to the left. Be careful to keep your upper body upright — you mustn't lean over to the left! Now, what happens as you turn to the left? Your left hand goes back, your right hand moves to the left, and suddenly your right leg is further back than your left. And, hey presto, you've taken up the inside rein, pushed on the girth with your inside leg and the outside leg is behind the girth — all quite automatically, and without pulling on the reins.

There's one thing missing. Do you know what it is? That's right — you have to look in the direction you want to ride in. Watch the other riders at your stable. Many of them will look down at their horse while they're riding in the arena. Well, why not? You're not suddenly going to come across a tree in your way in the school, nor will there be any other hazards, such as a car coming past. This is true, but don't forget that most of the time when you're in the arena you ride in patterns that rely on you turning away at certain markers and coming back at others. And, to be able to turn at the right time, you have to look where you want to go. It's quite simple, if you don't look anywhere, you won't go anywhere!

Another reason to look in the direction you want to ride in is that it automatically helps you turn your upper body, which you need to do to make the horse turn. For example, if you want to ride across the long diagonal, turn your head inwards after you go through the corner, so that you're looking at the marker in front of the opposite corner. And just let your upper body follow the direction of this turn. Your horse will feel the shift of weight, and turn with it. And, since you are looking straight at the change marker on the opposite side, the horse will ride straight to it.

Problems at the canter

Riding at the walk and trot is often easier than cantering. There are actually two different kinds of canter: when going clockwise, you ride a right-lead canter, and anticlockwise you ride a left-lead canter. Do you know the difference between them? Watch other riders when they're cantering, or watch the horses cantering on their own in the paddock. Look to see which foreleg reaches further forward. If it's the right leg, then that's the right-lead canter. If it's the left, the horse is in a left-lead canter.

So far, so good. But how do you get a horse to canter on left or right leads, and how can you tell which one it's doing when you're sitting on top? First think about the aids you need to use to ask a horse to canter (which your riding teacher should already have explained to you): your outside leg slides about a hand's breadth backwards, while your inside leg keeps its position on the saddle girth. You push a little harder with your inside leg. When your horse goes into canter, move your inside hand forward a little, so slackening the rein, to let him extend his stride. Only ever canter from a nice calm trot; don't rush your horse into a canter. If, when you ask your horse for canter, he simply goes into a faster trot, bring him back to a calm trot and ask again, this time maybe with the help of your whip.

Once your horse is cantering, look down and cast a quick glance at his shoulders — you can see really clearly from them which foreleg is reaching further forward and so whether the horse is in a left- or a right-lead canter. However, you should quickly learn how to feel this, rather than having to look, because you have to lean forward to do it, and that puts your horse out of balance. It is quite easy to feel whether the horse is in a left-lead or a right-lead canter. Ask your horse to canter anticlockwise. When he is cantering, count to yourself, 'Left, left, left...' Does it feel like left, left, left...? If it does then he is doing a left-lead canter, if not then he is on the wrong leg, and is doing a right-lead canter, even though you're cantering anticlockwise. Look at his shoulders and check if your feeling was right. Were you right? Well done! Take your horse back to a

Practical tip

HORSES PREFER LEFT-LEAD CANTER!

All horses have a side on which they would rather canter, just like us — we are either left-handed or right-handed. But most people are right-handed, whereas most horses prefer to canter in left-lead. If your horse refuses to canter on the side that's less comfortable for him, you can't force him to do so. That would be like suddenly forcing you to write with your wrong hand. You would be right to resist and so would he. But, imagine that someone worked to help you for a long time until you could write just as well with either hand, then that would be fine. The same applies to your horse. Ride him through turns and loops at walk and trot until he's just as strong and skilful on his 'bad side' as on his good one. When his muscles are equally well trained on both sides, he'll be able to canter properly on both sides.

nice calm trot and canter on again. Most well-trained horses automatically go into canter on the correct lead when they're in an arena, especially if you ask for canter on a corner.

But what if your horse won't canter on at all? Lazy horses often pretend that they have no idea what the canter aid means, and horses that have only just been broken in really don't know what it means. For both, you have to do the same thing. Give a clear canter aid, and if nothing happens, repeat the aid, giving the horse a light tap with the whip at the same time. Don't allow him to trot on faster. Make it clear that this was not what you asked for. Finally, have an image in your mind's eye of how you want the pair of you to be cantering. Slow up your horse again, and repeat the aid, including the tap with the whip, with more energy. With a lazy horse, though, this won't be enough. Once you're cantering, you'll need to go on giving your canter aid at every stride, otherwise the horse will just do the one canter stride that you asked for and then drop back to trot.

Now you know some of the secrets to making riding look so easy. If you learn the checklist below by heart and always follow it, you too will soon be one of those riders that everyone else admires.

FULFIL YOUR GOOD INTENTIONS

Checklist for your next riding session:

I must
- not pull the reins;
- first make an image in my mind of what I want the horse to do;
- 'sink into' the horse when I want to stop;
- turn my upper body in the direction I want the horse to go;
- look in the direction I want to ride in;
- learn to tell by feel whether I'm riding left-lead or right-lead canter.

Find the answers on page 77.

RIDER'S QUIZ ?

You'll find again and again that your horse doesn't understand what you want him to do, or that he just doesn't want to do it. Do you know what to do when each of these problems arises?

1. I want to turn, but my horse just bends his neck and walks straight on.

_____

_____

_____

2. My horse goes at a snail's pace, even though I'm driving him on so hard that my legs are nearly falling off.

_____

_____

_____

3. I want to stop, but my horse just pulls on the reins and goes on walking.

_____

_____

_____

4. My horse goes into canter, but falls back to a trot after only a few strides.

_____

_____

_____

Horses are not only different in their temperaments, but also in what they can be used for. Of course, most horses can be used for most things, but for some purposes there are particular breeds of horse that are better than others. So the kind of horse you should ride often depends on what discipline you're interested in.

This Arab is good at dressage, but you won't often see Arab horses at competitions.

Dressage and show jumping If you'd like to do the traditional disciplines of dressage and show jumping, and maybe take part in competitions, a warmblood-type is certainly the best kind of horse for you. An alternative, if you're small enough, would be an elegant pony that looks like a scaled-down version of a riding horse. But you must bear in mind that you'll only be allowed to compete on a pony as long as you qualify for the junior sections. Once you're older, you'll need to change to a bigger horse.

A warmblood is an excellent choice if you want to do show jumping.

Leisure riding   There's a bigger choice if your interests are many and varied — maybe you'd like to do some schoolwork occasionally in the arena, take part in gymkhanas, go for long rides with your friends and perhaps enter your club's annual show. If so, you need to ask yourself which of all of these you think is the most fun. Is it riding out with your friends? In this case you need a good, solid trail horse, but something that's not too big. What about one of the mountain and moorland breeds, such as a Welsh Cob, a Fell or Dales, or a Dartmoor pony? Or you could choose a nice, robust crossbreed. If the annual show is the most important thing to you, and you're going to be spending a lot of time preparing for dressage tests in the arena, then you ought to opt for something like a warmblood. Welsh or New Forest ponies would also be suitable, though, as they often find schoolwork more fun than heavier breeds.

Western riding   If you've learnt Western riding, you probably already know that the best breeds for this kind of riding are the three American breeds: the Quarter Horse, the Pinto or Paint, and the Appaloosa. But, as long as you're not hoping to win the Quarter Horse Reining Championships — this year! — you can do

Fjord horses make good Western horses too.

Western riding on quite an 'ordinary' horse. Just make sure that it isn't too big, because big horses are less agile than their smaller cousins. You should also be on the lookout for a horse with a short back, because stopping quickly (which is one of the elements of Western riding) is kinder on the hindquarters of short-backed horses. Arabs, Haflingers and lots of different kinds of ponies can make really good Western riding horses.

Riding gaited horses   Horses that have extra paces, or gaits, above and beyond walk, trot, canter and gallop, are called gaited horses. Gaits include the tölt, or running walk, and the flying pace. These extra gaits are wonderfully comfortable for you when you're sitting, because you don't get shaken about

Icelandic horses are much-loved gaited horses.

67

like you do in the trot. Among the best-known gaited horses are the Icelandic horse, the Tennessee Walker and the Peruvian Paso. Icelandics mature late, and ideally they shouldn't be broken in before the age of five.

Find the answers on pages 78—79.

GOING OUT FOR A RIDE

So you don't just want to ride in the arena — you want to get out there and ride through the countryside with your friends? In that case, there's a lot for you to remember. Do you know the most important rules for cross-country riding? Find out by doing this quiz!

1. How should I ride past pedestrians?

2. Am I allowed to ride on the pavement?

3. Can I lead my horse on roads where riding is forbidden?

4. Why shouldn't I trot too much on tarmac roads?

5. Am I allowed to gallop beside a pasture?

6. I'd like to ride across a field of stubble. Can I?

7. My friends ride too fast for me. Should I go on riding with them?

8. The last time we were on our favourite gallop, my horse bolted. What should I do?

9. When I ride out with my friends, I can't get my horse to go away from the group. What should I do?

VARIETY IN THE ARENA !

To do this exercise, place four or five buckets, cans or jump stands around the riding arena. This will help both you and your horse — it gives you an idea of where you should ride to, and it's much more meaningful for your horse to ride around an object than just to go round in some figure or other. In the middle of the arena, lay out two fence poles, one to 1-1.5 metres (3—5 feet) apart.

Exercise 1: Start at the first bucket. Ride in a walk to the next one, circle it anticlockwise, ride on to the next and halt beside it. Let your horse stand still while you count to five, then ride on. Circle the next bucket clockwise, and the last one anticlockwise again. To finish, ride through the corridor made by the two poles.

Once the exercise goes well at a walk, you can do it in a trot. Or, if you like, walk round the buckets and trot between them. Once you're confident enough you can even canter between the buckets. Of course, you don't always need to do the obstacles in the same order; varying the course will stop it from getting boring too quickly — otherwise many horses will learn the exercise by heart and will do it without waiting for your aids. To make it more difficult, you can try holding both reins in one hand and doing the exercise one-handed, Western-style.

Practical tip

Exercise 2: Here's an exercise for more advanced riders. Trot to the first bucket. Trot around it anticlockwise, stop by the next bucket, count to five and take your horse backwards for three steps. Out of the backward steps, trot on, stop by the next bucket and walk round it clockwise. Trot on again, and trot round the last bucket anticlockwise. Trot on through the pole corridor, halt at the end, let your horse stand still again while you count to five, then take him backwards between the poles. Then canter back to the first bucket.

Pretty difficult, wasn't it? Especially as it isn't a question of just hurtling round the buckets any old how. Always remember that the point of these exercises is to practise delicate aids. You'll have achieved this when people watching you would think that your horse is doing all of these changes of speed and direction by himself.

APPENDIX

Quiz answers

Test your horsemanship – Answers from pages 10–11

1. Answer c is right. The horse is used to the cat, and if he stops for a moment to look at it out of curiosity, he doesn't deserve to be punished with a tug on his halter.

2. Answer b is right. If a horse kicks the stable door with his forefoot, he's showing you that he isn't happy and wants to move around. So, the right solution is to give him more exercise. Tying him up in the stable will be just as pointless as shouting at him, because you aren't solving the problem.

3. Answer c is right. To raise a hoof, you press on the sinewy part of the horse's leg until he reacts. Hitting his leg or kicking him is far too rough and would frighten your horse.

4. Answer b is right. For your own safety, you must pull back if the horses start to close in on you. Do not feed them, otherwise the ones that don't get any food will get jealous and start to squabble. If that does happen, don't get between the horses. The same applies if you try to chase them away. If you make them shy, they might get so scared that they knock you down by mistake.

5. Answer b is right. If your horse refuses a fence, it's generally because the fence is too high — either for your horse or for you. Put the pole lower, so that you both gain confidence in what you can do. You should only punish a horse for a refusal if you are an experienced showjumper who can tell exactly why your horse will not jump. Shortening the left rein won't help either, because even if your horse's head is pulled to the left, he will still break out to the right.

This horse is looking expectantly over the stable door.

6. Answer b is right. It's just plain common sense that you should walk downhill. If you trot downhill, you can easily fall. Many horses will try to speed up going downhill. You must prevent them from doing this, as it is too dangerous.

What type is my horse? – Answers from page 19

Seven to nine 'yes' answers. Your horse is a real prima donna! If he's so fiery even when he isn't being ridden, this shows that it's just in his nature. It might be the cause of your riding problems too, but maybe the horse is just young, and that's why he shies so much. Make an effort to be very gentle when you're with him. Never run races with your friends on this horse!

Seven to nine 'sometimes' answers. Your horse is a clown. Do you think he might be bored? Maybe he shies occasionally during your riding sessions because he's trying to vary things a bit. But it's also possible that he's trying things on to see what he can get away with and what he can't. If this is the case, ride him on energetically, so that he knows which of you is the boss. When you're on this horse, don't daydream! Who knows what nonsense he's going to come up with next!

Seven to nine 'no' answers. Your horse is probably a reliable and uncomplicated horse. He's likely to be easy-going, maybe rather greedy and probably also fairly old. Such horses are perfect for learning how to ride. But make sure you impose your will on him, because once a horse like this gets the feeling that you aren't serious, from then on he will only move at a snail's pace — if at all!

An even mixture of 'yes', 'no' and 'sometimes'. Your horse is quite a normal horse, who shies sometimes and plays up sometimes, but calms down quickly again. If he only shows his temperamental side at certain times, try to find out why. Are there many days when he doesn't get out to the field? Does he get too much concentrated feed? Is he ridden often enough?

Can you recognize horse illnesses? – Answers from page 38

1. 'Colic' is a collective word for all kinds of stomach pains, and so colics can be very different. Typical symptoms of colic are that

Hooves need to
be cleaned
out regularly.

the horse looks around towards his stomach or kicks his hindleg towards his stomach, or that he carelessly throws himself to the ground and rolls about, or keeps lying down.

2. If you suspect colic you must immediately call the vet! Then, if it is safe, you can try to distract him a little by leading him around. But if he is thrashing about with the pain, keep away — he might hurt you without meaning to!

3. The normal body temperature is between 37.5 and 38.2 °C (99.5 and 100 °F), and is measured by inserting the thermometer in the rectum.

4. If your horse has a cough, take his temperature! If he doesn't have a high temperature, make sure that he's getting plenty of fresh air. If the cough hasn't cleared up after two days, call the vet — but if he has a high temperature, call the vet at once.

5. Injections protect against illnesses like flu, rabies and tetanus.

Regular worming is important.

The most important is the tetanus injection, because horses can catch this disease very easily. It comes from bacteria in the soil and infects them through cuts or even broken skin — and it is fatal. The injection must be repeated every two years. Flu injections are also important, especially if you plan to take your horse to shows.

6. Four to six wormings a year is usually enough.

7. Lameness is easiest to recognize when your horse is trotting. If he's lame in a foreleg, he will nod his head clearly when he treads on the lame leg during the trot. You need to look more carefully to spot lameness in a hindleg. Ask someone to lead the horse away from you in a trot. Then you'll see if he's taking normal strides with one leg and noticeably shorter ones with the other. If your horse is lame, first check to see if he has a stone or other object in his hoof — if he does you can get it out with a hoof pick. If there is no stone to be found, you need to call the vet so that he can treat the lame leg.

8. If your horse's back is wet, you don't need to miss out on riding. But if he's been rolling and is covered in soil or sand, you must carefully brush all the grains away from around the saddle and girth areas, so that there's nothing left to scratch or rub him.

9. Because you clean your horse's hooves every day, you'll easily see when they are getting too long or if pieces of horn are broken off. If your horse is shod, check his shoes. You'll need to call the farrier if they are worn thin or if they're loose or broken. But, even if they look fine, you should call the farrier every six to eight weeks to take the shoes off, cut the horn back and fit new shoes.

Rider's quiz –
Answers from page 64

1. I've pulled too hard on the inside rein and completely forgotten to turn my body in the direction I want to turn in. Of course, I must also remember to press with my inside leg.

2. I should give light leg aids and support them with the whip, until my horse has learnt to obey light leg pressure. After all, riding is not a trial of strength!

3. Oh dear, I've been pulling again! I need to have my hands quite still and quiet, and stop following the movements of the horse. Then my horse will stop at once.

4. I got so excited about him going into a canter that I completely forgot to go on driving him on. In future I need to remember to 'ride out' every single canter pace.

Going out for a ride –
Answers from page 68

1. Ride past pedestrians at a walk. And if you say a friendly 'Hello!' as you're going by, most pedestrians will be pleasantly surprised.

2. It's illegal to ride on the pavement. You must use the road.

3. If riding is banned on a particular road, then so is leading your horse on it. The road sign might show a rider sitting on the horse, but the meaning of the sign is not 'No riding!' but 'No horses!'.

4. Unlike tracks made of natural things, tarmac roads don't 'give' when a horse steps on them. If you trot on a tarmac road, the hard impact on the horse's hooves goes straight up into his legs, and that can make him go lame.

5. When you go past fields that contain horses, cows or other animals, you should only walk. Otherwise, the pasture animals might start running along with you, and they could get so excited that when they get to the end of the field, they run into the fence instead of stopping. Even if they don't run with you, they might take fright and injure themselves.

6. It's great fun to gallop across stubble fields. But you can only ride through fields if you have permission from whoever owns them.

7. If you get scared every time you go out riding because your friends are always racing each other, you should ask them to be more considerate. If they don't want to be more understanding, you'll be better off finding other friends to ride with.

8. Your horse knows your favourite gallop just as well as you do! He knows that you always gallop on this track and so he's ready and excited before you even ask him to go. For the next few weeks, don't gallop here. Ride at walk and trot instead so that he learns that he doesn't always get to gallop along this bit and that he has to change his pace from fast to slow on this stretch too. Once that's working well, canter on for a bit and then change speeds again.

9. Your horse feels safe in the group. He 'sticks' socially to the other horses. To show him that he doesn't need to be scared on his own either, begin by riding at the head of the group for a while. If he doesn't want to go at the front on his own, ask one of the other riders to come with you, keeping their horse's head around the level of your knee. Another helpful exercise is riding away and waiting. Ask another rider to trot away from the group and wait for you a short distance away. Then you go to join them; this way you'll be leaving the others to catch up with another horse.